THE GOSPEL IS THE POWER OF GOD UNTO SALVATION

THE GOSPEL IS THE POWER OF GOD UNTO SALVATION

Compiled by Eugene Carvalho

The Gospel Is the Power of God Unto Salvation

Copyright © 2019 by Eugene Carvalho

ISBN: 9781091934801

Printed in the United States of America

"Scripture taken from the
NEW AMERICAN STANDARD BIBLE ®
Copyright ©
1960,1962,1963,1968,1971,1972,1973,1975,1977,1995
by The Lockman Foundation. Used by permission."

Scripture quotations from The Authorized (King James) Version. Rights in the Authorized Version in the United Kingdom are vested in the Crown. Reproduced by permission of the Crown's patentee, Cambridge University Press

To the Body of Christ.
May this compilation bless you richly!
With love…

TABLE OF CONTENTS

PURPOSE AND ACKNOWLEDGEMENTS

The infallible Word of God for faith and conduct informs us that the Holy Spirit gives gifts to men and women of the Body of Christ. It states: "the gifts edify the body for the building up of the saints" (Eph. 4:12). I hope the talents and gifts the Lord has given me will be a blessing to someone else through the reading of this compilation.

I am grateful for the love I have received from family members, especially my wife Mercedes Carvalho. I am also grateful for the knowledge, wisdom and love of many pastors, teachers, and saints that the Lord has used to bless me. Lastly, I must not forget a special thank you to my friend Kathryn Regan for proofreading this material.

Chapter One
THE GOSPEL

The Greek word *euaggelion*, which was translated "gospel" is found in about seventy-five verses depending on the version of the Bible you're using. The word gospel literally means "good tidings," and/or "good news."

Jesus preached the pure gospel of the kingdom under the power of the Holy Spirit, so didn't Peter, Stephen and the apostle Paul. They were able to turn the world up-side-down preaching with such convicting power. Their adversaries hated the power of God so much they had all but one disciple murdered.

It saddens me that the modern church has managed to present the gospel in such a perverted way, no one is really willing to die for it. Many won't travel into hostile third world countries to preach. They leave the church and watch football all day long. Some churches have become like social clubs. They have watered down the gospel to make it seeker-friendly. Many churches have stepped over the line and have come into agreement on issues like homosexuality, abortion and other vital issues even though God's Word is very clear on such issues.

The Bibles says, "For the word of God is quick, and powerful, and sharper than any twoedged sword, piercing even to the dividing asunder of soul and spirit, and of the joints and marrow, and is a discerner of the thoughts and intents of the heart" (Heb. 4:12 KJV).

From that verse we learn it's only through the gospel an individual can lay aside the old man. Paul stated, "But you did not learn Christ in this way, if indeed you have heard Him and have been taught in Him, just as truth is in Jesus, that, in reference to your former manner of life, you lay aside the old self, which is being corrupted in accordance with the lusts of deceit, and that you be renewed in the spirit of your mind, and put on the new self, which in the likeness of God has been created in righteousness and holiness of the truth" (Eph. 4:20-24).

Let me break down those verses for you. Faith comes by hearing the gospel. In the process your mind gets renewed by hearing it. If the mind is not renewed by the gospel lust will deceive you back into sin (the old man). James wrote, "But each one is tempted when he is carried away and enticed by his own lust. Then when lust has conceived, it gives birth to sin; and when sin is accomplished, it brings forth death" (Jas. 1:14-15).

Therefore, we meditate on the gospel in the morning and our mind gets renewed. The power of the Holy Spirit, through the preached gospel, gets the old person out of the way. The new man is then led by the Holy Spirit to be in the right place at the right time, to receive God's blessings.

When an individual is born-again their spirit is recreated. They become the righteousness of God in Christ. However, the mind needs to be renewed daily. The Bible says, "And do not be conformed to this world, but be transformed by the renewing of your mind, that you may prove what the will of God is, that which is good and acceptable and perfect" (Ro. 12:2). With that being said, let's investigate a vast array of scriptures that discuss the gospel.

Chapter Two

THE GOSPEL IN THE NEW TESTAMENT

IN THE BOOK OF MATTHEW

Jesus Was Proclaiming the Gospel

"Jesus was going throughout all Galilee, teaching in their synagogues and proclaiming the gospel of the kingdom, and healing every kind of disease and every kind of sickness among the people. The news about Him spread throughout all Syria; and they brought to Him all who were ill, those suffering with various diseases and pains, demoniacs, epileptics, paralytics; and He healed them. Large crowds followed Him from Galilee and the Decapolis and Jerusalem and Judea and from beyond the Jordan" (Mt. 4:23-25).

The Gospel of the Kingdom

"Jesus was going through all the cities and villages, teaching in their synagogues and proclaiming the gospel of the kingdom, and healing every kind of disease and every kind of sickness. Seeing the people, He felt compassion for them, because they were distressed and dispirited like sheep without a shepherd. Then He said to His disciples, 'The harvest is plentiful, but the workers are few. Therefore beseech the Lord of the harvest to send out workers into His harvest'" (Mt. 9:35-38).

Chapter Two

The Poor Have the Gospel Preached to Them

"Now when John, while imprisoned, heard of the works of Christ, he sent word by his disciples and said to Him, 'Are You the Expected One, or shall we look for someone else?' Jesus answered and said to them, 'Go and report to John what you hear and see: the BLIND RECEIVE SIGHT and the lame walk, the lepers are cleansed and the deaf hear, the dead are raised up, and the POOR HAVE THE GOSPEL PREACHED TO THEM. And blessed is he who does not take offense at Me'" (Mt. 11:2-6).

This Gospel of the Kingdom Shall Be Preached in the Whole World

"Then they will deliver you to tribulation, and will kill you, and you will be hated by all nations because of My name. At that time many will fall away and will betray one another and hate one another. Many false prophets will arise and will mislead many. Because lawlessness is increased, most people's love will grow cold. But the one who endures to the end, he will be saved. This gospel of the kingdom shall be preached in the whole world as a testimony to all the nations, and then the end will come" (Mt. 24:9-14).

Wherever This Gospel Is Preached

"Now when Jesus was in Bethany, at the home of Simon the leper, a woman came to Him with an alabaster vial of very costly perfume, and she poured it on His head as He reclined at the table.

Chapter Two

But the disciples were indignant when they saw this, and said, 'Why this waste? For this perfume might have been sold for a high price and the money given to the poor.' But Jesus, aware of this, said to them, 'Why do you bother the woman? For she has done a good deed to Me. For you always have the poor with you; but you do not always have Me. For when she poured this perfume on My body, she did it to prepare Me for burial. Truly I say to you, wherever this gospel is preached in the whole world, what this woman has done will also be spoken of in memory of her'" (Mt. 26:6-13).

IN THE BOOK OF MARK

The Gospel of Jesus Christ, the Son of God

"The beginning of the gospel of Jesus Christ, the Son of God. As it is written in Isaiah the prophet: 'BEHOLD, I SEND MY MESSENGER AHEAD OF YOU, WHO WILL PREPARE YOUR WAY; THE VOICE OF ONE CRYING IN THE WILDERNESS, "MAKE READY THE WAY OF THE LORD, MAKE HIS PATHS STRAIGHT.'" John the Baptist appeared in the wilderness preaching a baptism of repentance for the forgiveness of sins. And all the country of Judea was going out to him, and all the people of Jerusalem; and they were being baptized by him in the Jordan River, confessing their sins. John was clothed with camel's hair and wore a leather belt around his waist, and his diet was locusts and wild honey. And he was preaching, and saying, 'After me One is coming who is mightier than I, and I am not fit to stoop down and untie the thong of His sandals.

Chapter Two

I baptized you with water; but He will baptize you with the Holy Spirit'" (Mk. 1:1-8).

Repent and Believe in the Gospel

"Now after John had been taken into custody, Jesus came into Galilee, preaching the gospel of God, and saying, 'The time is fulfilled, and the kingdom of God is at hand; repent and believe in the gospel'" (Mk. 1:14-15).

Whoever Loses His Life for My Sake and the Gospel's Shall Save It

"And He summoned the crowd with His disciples, and said to them, 'If anyone wishes to come after Me, he must deny himself, and take up his cross and follow Me. For whoever wishes to save his life will lose it, but whoever loses his life for My sake and the gospel's will save it. For what does it profit a man to gain the whole world, and forfeit his soul? For what will a man give in exchange for his soul? For whoever is ashamed of Me and My words in this adulterous and sinful generation, the Son of Man will also be ashamed of him when He comes in the glory of His Father with the holy angels" (Mk. 8:34-38).

Left House or Brothers or Sisters or Mother or Father or Children or Farms, for the Gospel's Sake

"Peter began to say to Him, 'Behold, we have left everything and followed You.' Jesus said, 'Truly I say to you, there is no one who has left house or brothers or sisters or mother or father or children or farms, for My sake and for the gospel's sake, but that he will receive a hundred times as much now in the present age, houses and brothers and sisters and mothers and children and farms, along with persecutions; and in the age to come, eternal life. But many who are first will be last, and the last, first'" (Mk. 10:28-31).

The Gospel Must First Be Preached to All the Nations

"But be on your guard; for they will deliver you to the courts, and you will be flogged in the synagogues, and you will stand before governors and kings for My sake, as a testimony to them. The gospel must first be preached to all the nations. When they arrest you and hand you over, do not worry beforehand about what you are to say, but say whatever is given you in that hour; for it is not you who speak, but it is the Holy Spirit. Brother will betray brother to death, and a father his child; and children will rise up against parents and have them put to death. You will be hated by all because of My name, but the one who endures to the end, he will be saved" (Mk. 13:9-13).

Wherever the Gospel Is Preached

"While He was in Bethany at the home of Simon the leper, and reclining at the table, there came a woman with an alabaster vial of very costly perfume of pure nard; and she broke the vial and poured it over His head. But some were indignantly remarking to one another, 'Why has this perfume been wasted? For this perfume might have been sold for over three hundred denarii, and the money given to the poor.' And they were scolding her. But Jesus said, 'Let her alone; why do you bother her? She has done a good deed to Me. For you always have the poor with you, and whenever you wish you can do good to them; but you do not always have Me. She has done what she could; she has anointed My body beforehand for the burial. Truly I say to you, wherever the gospel is preached in the whole world, what this woman has done will also be spoken of in memory of her'" (Mk. 14:3-9).

Go into All the World and Preach the Gospel to All Creation

"Afterward He appeared to the eleven themselves as they were reclining at the table; and He reproached them for their unbelief and hardness of heart, because they had not believed those who had seen Him after He had risen. And He said to them, 'Go into all the world and preach the gospel to all creation. He who has believed and has been baptized shall be saved; but he who has disbelieved shall be condemned. These signs will accompany those who have believed: in My name they will cast out demons, they will speak with new tongues; they will pick up serpents, and if they drink any deadly poison, it will not hurt them; they will lay hands on the sick, and they will recover'" (Mk. 16:14-18).

Chapter Two

IN THE BOOK OF LUKE

He Preached the Gospel to the People

"So with many other exhortations he preached the gospel to the people. But when Herod the tetrarch was reprimanded by him because of Herodias, his brother's wife, and because of all the wicked things which Herod had done, Herod also added this to them all: he locked John up in prison" (Lk. 3:18-20).

He Anointed Me to Preach the Gospel to the Poor

"And He came to Nazareth, where He had been brought up; and as was His custom, He entered the synagogue on the Sabbath, and stood up to read. And the book of the prophet Isaiah was handed to Him. And He opened the book and found the place where it was written, 'THE SPIRIT OF THE LORD IS UPON ME, BECAUSE HE ANOINTED ME TO PREACH THE GOSPEL TO THE POOR. HE HAS SENT ME TO PROCLAIM RELEASE TO THE CAPTIVES, AND RECOVERY OF SIGHT TO THE BLIND, TO SET FREE THOSE WHO ARE OPPRESSED, TO PROCLAIM THE FAVORABLE YEAR OF THE LORD.' And He closed the book, gave it back to the attendant and sat down; and the eyes of all in the synagogue were fixed on Him. And He began to say to them, 'Today this Scripture has been fulfilled in your hearing.' And all were speaking well of Him, and wondering at the gracious words which were falling from His lips; and they were saying, 'Is this not Joseph's son?'

Chapter Two

And He said to them, 'No doubt you will quote this proverb to Me, "Physician, heal yourself! Whatever we heard was done at Capernaum, do here in your hometown as well."' And He said, 'Truly I say to you, no prophet is welcome in his hometown. But I say to you in truth, there were many widows in Israel in the days of Elijah, when the sky was shut up for three years and six months, when a great famine came over all the land; and yet Elijah was sent to none of them, but only to Zarephath, in the land of Sidon, to a woman who was a widow. And there were many lepers in Israel in the time of Elisha the prophet; and none of them was cleansed, but only Naaman the Syrian.' And all the people in the synagogue were filled with rage as they heard these things; and they got up and drove Him out of the city, and led Him to the brow of the hill on which their city had been built, in order to throw Him down the cliff. But passing through their midst, He went His way" (Lk. 4:16-30).

Tell John the Poor Have the Gospel Preached to Them

"The disciples of John reported to him about all these things. Summoning two of his disciples, John sent them to the Lord, saying, 'Are You the Expected One, or do we look for someone else?' When the men came to Him, they said, 'John the Baptist has sent us to You, to ask, "Are You the Expected One, or do we look for someone else?"' At that very time He cured many people of diseases and afflictions and evil spirits; and He gave sight to many who were blind. And He answered and said to them, 'Go and report to John what you have seen and heard: the BLIND RECEIVE SIGHT, the lame walk, the lepers are cleansed, and the deaf hear, the dead are raised up, the POOR HAVE THE GOSPEL PREACHED TO THEM. Blessed is he who does not take offense at Me'" (Lk. 7:18-23).

Preaching the Gospel, and Healing Everywhere

"And He called the twelve together, and gave them power and authority over all the demons and to heal diseases. And He sent them out to proclaim the kingdom of God and to perform healing. And He said to them, 'Take nothing for your journey, neither a staff, nor a bag, nor bread, nor money; and do not even have two tunics apiece. Whatever house you enter, stay there until you leave that city. And as for those who do not receive you, as you go out from that city, shake the dust off your feet as a testimony against them.' Departing, they began going throughout the villages, preaching the gospel and healing everywhere" (Lk. 9:1-6).

Since Then the Gospel of the Kingdom of God Is Preached

"The Law and the Prophets were proclaimed until John; since that time the gospel of the kingdom of God has been preached, and everyone is forcing his way into it. But it is easier for heaven and earth to pass away than for one stroke of a letter of the Law to fail" (Lk. 16:16-17).

Chapter Two

Teaching and Preaching the Gospel in the Temple

"On one of the days while He was teaching the people in the temple and preaching the gospel, the chief priests and the scribes with the elders confronted Him, and they spoke, saying to Him, 'Tell us by what authority You are doing these things, or who is the one who gave You this authority?' Jesus answered and said to them, 'I will also ask you a question, and you tell Me: Was the baptism of John from heaven or from men?' They reasoned among themselves, saying, 'If we say, "From heaven," He will say, "Why did you not believe him?" But if we say, "From men," all the people will stone us to death, for they are convinced that John was a prophet.' So they answered that they did not know where it came from. And Jesus said to them, 'Nor will I tell you by what authority I do these things'" (Lk. 20:1-8).

IN THE BOOK OF ACTS

Preaching the Gospel to Many Villages

"So, when they had solemnly testified and spoken the word of the Lord, they started back to Jerusalem, and were preaching the gospel to many villages of the Samaritans. But an angel of the Lord spoke to Philip saying, 'Get up and go south to the road that descends from Jerusalem to Gaza.' (This is a desert road.) So he got up and went; and there was an Ethiopian eunuch, a court official of Candace, queen of the Ethiopians, who was in charge of all her treasure; and he had come to Jerusalem to worship,

Chapter Two

and he was returning and sitting in his chariot, and was reading the prophet Isaiah. Then the Spirit said to Philip, 'Go up and join this chariot.' Philip ran up and heard him reading Isaiah the prophet, and said, 'Do you understand what you are reading?' And he said, 'Well, how could I, unless someone guides me?' And he invited Philip to come up and sit with him. Now the passage of Scripture which he was reading was this: 'HE WAS LED AS A SHEEP TO SLAUGHTER; AND AS A LAMB BEFORE ITS SHEARER IS SILENT, SO HE DOES NOT OPEN HIS MOUTH. IN HUMILIATION HIS JUDGMENT WAS TAKEN AWAY; WHO WILL RELATE HIS GENERATION? FOR HIS LIFE IS REMOVED FROM THE EARTH.' The eunuch answered Philip and said, 'Please tell me, of whom does the prophet say this? Of himself or of someone else?' Then Philip opened his mouth, and beginning from this Scripture he preached Jesus to him. As they went along the road they came to some water; and the eunuch said, 'Look! Water! What prevents me from being baptized?' And Philip said, 'If you believe with all your heart, you may.' And he answered and said, 'I believe that Jesus Christ is the Son of God.' And he ordered the chariot to stop; and they both went down into the water, Philip as well as the eunuch, and he baptized him. When they came up out of the water, the Spirit of the Lord snatched Philip away; and the eunuch no longer saw him, but went on his way rejoicing. But Philip found himself at Azotus, and as he passed through he kept preaching the gospel to all the cities until he came to Caesarea" (Ac. 8:25-40).

Chapter Two

And There They Continued to Preach the Gospel

"In Iconium they entered the synagogue of the Jews together, and spoke in such a manner that a large number of people believed, both of Jews and of Greeks. But the Jews who disbelieved stirred up the minds of the Gentiles and embittered them against the brethren. Therefore they spent a long time there speaking boldly with reliance upon the Lord, who was testifying to the word of His grace, granting that signs and wonders be done by their hands. But the people of the city were divided; and some sided with the Jews, and some with the apostles. And when an attempt was made by both the Gentiles and the Jews with their rulers, to mistreat and to stone them, they became aware of it and fled to the cities of Lycaonia, Lystra and Derbe, and the surrounding region; and there they continued to preach the gospel" (Ac. 14:1-7).

We Preach the Gospel to You so You Can Turn from These Vain Things to a Living God

"At Lystra a man was sitting who had no strength in his feet, lame from his mother's womb, who had never walked. This man was listening to Paul as he spoke, who, when he had fixed his gaze on him and had seen that he had faith to be made well, said with a loud voice, 'Stand upright on your feet.' And he leaped up and began to walk. When the crowds saw what Paul had done, they raised their voice, saying in the Lycaonian language, 'The gods have become like men and have come down to us.' And they began calling Barnabas, Zeus, and

Paul, Hermes, because he was the chief speaker. The priest of Zeus, whose temple was just outside the city, brought oxen and garlands to the gates, and wanted to offer sacrifice with the crowds. But when the apostles Barnabas and Paul heard of it, they tore their robes and rushed out into the crowd, crying out and saying, 'Men, why are you doing these things? We are also men of the same nature as you, and preach the gospel to you that you should turn from these vain things to a living God, WHO MADE THE HEAVEN AND THE EARTH AND THE SEA AND ALL THAT IS IN THEM. In the generations gone by He permitted all the nations to go their own ways; and yet He did not leave Himself without witness, in that He did good and gave you rains from heaven and fruitful seasons, satisfying your hearts with food and gladness.' Even saying these things, with difficulty they restrained the crowds from offering sacrifice to them" (Ac. 14:8-18).

They Preached the Gospel to that City and Had Made Many Disciples

"But Jews came from Antioch and Iconium, and having won over the crowds, they stoned Paul and dragged him out of the city, supposing him to be dead. But while the disciples stood around him, he got up and entered the city. The next day he went away with Barnabas to Derbe. After they had preached the gospel to that city and had made many disciples, they returned to Lystra and to Iconium and to Antioch, strengthening the souls of the disciples, encouraging them to continue in the faith, and saying, 'Through many tribulations we must enter the kingdom of God.' When they had appointed elders for them in every church, having prayed with fasting, they commended them to the Lord in whom they had believed" (Ac. 14:19-23).

The Gentiles Should Hear the Word of the Gospel and Believe

"The apostles and the elders came together to look into this matter. After there had been much debate, Peter stood up and said to them, 'Brethren, you know that in the early days God made a choice among you, that by my mouth the Gentiles would hear the word of the gospel and believe. And God, who knows the heart, testified to them giving them the Holy Spirit, just as He also did to us; and He made no distinction between us and them, cleansing their hearts by faith. Now therefore why do you put God to the test by placing upon the neck of the disciples a yoke which neither our fathers nor we have been able to bear? But we believe that we are saved through the grace of the Lord Jesus, in the same way as they also are'" (Ac. 15:6-11).

God Had Called Us to Preach the Gospel to Them

"They passed through the Phrygian and Galatian region, having been forbidden by the Holy Spirit to speak the word in Asia; and after they came to Mysia, they were trying to go into Bithynia, and the Spirit of Jesus did not permit them; and passing by Mysia, they came down to Troas. A vision appeared to Paul in the night: a man of Macedonia was standing and appealing to him, and saying,

Chapter Two

'Come over to Macedonia and help us.' When he had seen the vision, immediately we sought to go into Macedonia, concluding that God had called us to preach the gospel to them" (Ac. 16:6-10).

To Testify Solemnly of the Gospel of the Grace of God

"From Miletus he sent to Ephesus and called to him the elders of the church. And when they had come to him, he said to them, 'You yourselves know, from the first day that I set foot in Asia, how I was with you the whole time, serving the Lord with all humility and with tears and with trials which came upon me through the plots of the Jews; how I did not shrink from declaring to you anything that was profitable, and teaching you publicly and from house to house, solemnly testifying to both Jews and Greeks of repentance toward God and faith in our Lord Jesus Christ. And now, behold, bound in spirit, I am on my way to Jerusalem, not knowing what will happen to me there, except that the Holy Spirit solemnly testifies to me in every city, saying that bonds and afflictions await me. But I do not consider my life of any account as dear to myself, so that I may finish my course and the ministry which I received from the Lord Jesus, to testify solemnly of the gospel of the grace of God (Ac. 20:17-24).

Chapter Two
IN THE BOOK OF ROMANS

Paul an Apostle, Set Apart for the Gospel of God

"Paul, a bond-servant of Christ Jesus, called as an apostle, set apart for the gospel of God, which He promised beforehand through His prophets in the holy Scriptures, concerning His Son, who was born of a descendant of David according to the flesh, who was declared the Son of God with power by the resurrection from the dead, according to the Spirit of holiness, Jesus Christ our Lord, through whom we have received grace and apostleship to bring about the obedience of faith among all the Gentiles for His name's sake, among whom you also are the called of Jesus Christ" (Ro. 1:1-6).

I Serve in My Spirit in the Preaching of the Gospel

'First, I thank my God through Jesus Christ for you all, because your faith is being proclaimed throughout the whole world. For God, whom I serve in my spirit in the preaching of the gospel of His Son, is my witness as to how unceasingly I make mention of you, always in my prayers making request, if perhaps now at last by the will of God I may succeed in coming to you. For I long to see you so that I may impart some spiritual gift to you, that you may be established; that is, that I may be encouraged together with you while among you, each of us by the other's faith, both yours and mine. I do not want you to be unaware, brethren, that often I have planned to come to you (and have been prevented so far) so that I may obtain some fruit among you also, even as among the rest of the Gentiles. I am under obligation both to Greeks and to barbarians, both to the wise and to the foolish. So, for my part, I am eager to preach the gospel to you also who are in Rome" (Ro. 1:8-15).

I am Not Ashamed of the Gospel, for it Is the Power of God for Salvation

"For I am not ashamed of the gospel, for it is the power of God for salvation to everyone who believes, to the Jew first and also to the Greek. For in it the righteousness of God is revealed from faith to faith; as it is written, 'BUT THE RIGHTEOUS man SHALL LIVE BY FAITH'" (Ro. 1:16-17).

According to My Gospel

"For all who have sinned without the Law will also perish without the Law, and all who have sinned under the Law will be judged by the Law; for it is not the hearers of the Law who are just before God, but the doers of the Law will be justified. For when Gentiles who do not have the Law do instinctively the things of the Law, these, not having the Law, are a law to themselves, in that they show the work of the Law written in their hearts, their conscience bearing witness and their thoughts alternately accusing or else defending them, on the day when, according to my gospel, God will judge the secrets of men through Christ Jesus" (Ro. 2:12-16).

Chapter Two

From the Standpoint of the Gospel They Are Enemies

"For I do not want you, brethren, to be uninformed of this mystery—so that you will not be wise in your own estimation—that a partial hardening has happened to Israel until the fullness of the Gentiles has come in; and so all Israel will be saved; just as it is written, 'THE DELIVERER WILL COME FROM ZION, HE WILL REMOVE UNGODLINESS FROM JACOB. THIS IS MY COVENANT WITH THEM, WHEN I TAKE AWAY THEIR SINS.' From the standpoint of the gospel they are enemies for your sake, but from the standpoint of God's choice they are beloved for the sake of the fathers; for the gifts and the calling of God are irrevocable. For just as you once were disobedient to God, but now have been shown mercy because of their disobedience, so these also now have been disobedient, that because of the mercy shown to you they also may now be shown mercy. For God has shut up all in disobedience so that He may show mercy to all" (Ro. 11:25-32).

Ministering as a Priest the Gospel of God

"And concerning you, my brethren, I myself also am convinced that you yourselves are full of goodness, filled with all knowledge and able also to admonish one another. But I have written very boldly to you on some points so as to remind you again, because of the grace that was given me from God, to be a minister of Christ Jesus to the Gentiles, ministering as a priest the gospel of God, so that my offering of the Gentiles may become acceptable, sanctified by the Holy Spirit. Therefore in Christ Jesus I have found reason for boasting in things pertaining to God. For I will not presume to speak of anything except what Christ has accomplished through me, resulting in the obedience of the Gentiles by word and deed, in the power of signs and wonders, in the power of the Spirit; so that from Jerusalem and round about as far as Illyricum I have fully preached the gospel of Christ. And thus I aspired to preach the gospel, not where Christ was already named, so that I would not build on another man's foundation; but as it is written, 'THEY WHO HAD NO NEWS OF HIM SHALL SEE, AND THEY WHO HAVE NOT HEARD SHALL UNDERSTAND'" (Ro. 15:14-21).

Who Is Able to Establish You According to My Gospel

"Now to Him who is able to establish you according to my gospel and the preaching of Jesus Christ, according to the revelation of the mystery which has been kept secret for long ages past, but now is manifested, and by the Scriptures of the prophets, according to the commandment of the eternal God, has been made known to all the nations, leading to obedience of faith; to the only wise God, through Jesus Christ, be the glory forever. Amen" (Ro. 16:25-27).

Chapter Two

IN THE BOOK OF 1 CORINTHIANS

To Preach the Gospel, Not in Cleverness of Speech

"Now I exhort you, brethren, by the name of our Lord Jesus Christ, that you all agree and that there be no divisions among you, but that you be made complete in the same mind and in the same judgment. For I have been informed concerning you, my brethren, by Chloe's people, that there are quarrels among you. Now I mean this, that each one of you is saying, 'I am of Paul,' and 'I of Apollos,' and 'I of Cephas,' and 'I of Christ.' Has Christ been divided? Paul was not crucified for you, was he? Or were you baptized in the name of Paul? I thank God that I baptized none of you except Crispus and Gaius, so that no one would say you were baptized in my name. Now I did baptize also the household of Stephanas; beyond that, I do not know whether I baptized any other. For Christ did not send me to baptize, but to preach the gospel, not in cleverness of speech, so that the cross of Christ would not be made void" (1Co. 1:10-17).

I Became Your Father Through the Gospel

"I do not write these things to shame you, but to admonish you as my beloved children. For if you were to have countless tutors in Christ, yet you would not have many fathers, for in Christ Jesus I became your father through the gospel. Therefore I exhort you, be imitators of me. For this reason I have sent to you Timothy, who is my beloved and faithful child in the Lord, and he will remind you of my ways which are in Christ, just as I teach everywhere in every church. Now some have become arrogant, as though I were not coming to you. But I will come to you soon, if the Lord wills, and I shall find out, not the words of those who are arrogant but their power. For the kingdom of God does not consist in words but in power. What do you desire? Shall I come to you with a rod, or with love and a spirit of gentleness" (1Co. 4:14-21)?

We May Cause No Hindrance to the Gospel of Christ

"I am not speaking these things according to human judgment, am I? Or does not the Law also say these things? For it is written in the Law of Moses, 'YOU SHALL NOT MUZZLE THE OX WHILE HE IS THRESHING.' God is not concerned about oxen, is He? Or is He speaking altogether for our sake? Yes, for our sake it was written, because the plowman ought to plow in hope, and the thresher to thresh in hope of sharing the crops. If we sowed spiritual things in you, is it too much if we reap material things from you? If others share the right over you, do we not more? Nevertheless, we did not use this right, but we endure all things so that we will cause no hindrance to the gospel of Christ. Do you not know that those who perform sacred services eat the food of the temple, and those who attend regularly to the altar have their share from the altar? So also the Lord directed those who proclaim the gospel to get their living from the gospel" (1Co. 9:8-14).

Chapter Two

I May Offer the Gospel Without Charge

"But I have used none of these things. And I am not writing these things so that it will be done so in my case; for it would be better for me to die than have any man make my boast an empty one. For if I preach the gospel, I have nothing to boast of, for I am under compulsion; for woe is me if I do not preach the gospel. For if I do this voluntarily, I have a reward; but if against my will, I have a stewardship entrusted to me. What then is my reward? That, when I preach the gospel, I may offer the gospel without charge, so as not to make full use of my right in the gospel" (1Co. 9:15-18).

I Do All Things for the Sake of the Gospel

"For though I am free from all men, I have made myself a slave to all, so that I may win more. To the Jews I became as a Jew, so that I might win Jews; to those who are under the Law, as under the Law though not being myself under the Law, so that I might win those who are under the Law; to those who are without law, as without law, though not being without the law of God but under the law of Christ, so that I might win those who are without law. To the weak I became weak, that I might win the weak; I have become all things to all men, so that I may by all means save some. I do all things for the sake of the gospel, so that I may become a fellow partaker of it" (1Co. 9:19-23).

Chapter Two

I Make Known to You, Brethren, the Gospel

"Now I make known to you, brethren, the gospel which I preached to you, which also you received, in which also you stand, by which also you are saved, if you hold fast the word which I preached to you, unless you believed in vain" (1Co. 15:1-2).

IN THE BOOK OF 2 CORINTHIANS

I Came to Troas for the Gospel of Christ

"Now when I came to Troas for the gospel of Christ and when a door was opened for me in the Lord, I had no rest for my spirit, not finding Titus my brother; but taking my leave of them, I went on to Macedonia" (2Co. 2:12-13).

The Gospel Is Veiled to Those Who Are Perishing

"Therefore, since we have this ministry, as we received mercy, we do not lose heart, but we have renounced the things hidden because of shame, not walking in craftiness or adulterating the word of God, but by the manifestation of truth commending ourselves to every man's conscience in the sight of God. And even if our gospel is veiled, it is veiled to those who are perishing, in whose case the god of this world has blinded the minds of the unbelieving so that they might not see the light of the gospel of the glory of Christ, who is the image of God. For we do not preach ourselves but Christ Jesus as Lord, and ourselves as your bond-servants for Jesus' sake.

Chapter Two

For God, who said, 'Light shall shine out of darkness,' is the One who has shone in our hearts to give the Light of the knowledge of the glory of God in the face of Christ" (2Co. 4:1-6).

The Things of the Gospel Has Spread Through All the Churches

"But thanks be to God who puts the same earnestness on your behalf in the heart of Titus. For he not only accepted our appeal, but being himself very earnest, he has gone to you of his own accord. We have sent along with him the brother whose fame in the things of the gospel has spread through all the churches; and not only this, but he has also been appointed by the churches to travel with us in this gracious work, which is being administered by us for the glory of the Lord Himself, and to show our readiness, taking precaution so that no one will discredit us in our administration of this generous gift; for we have regard for what is honorable, not only in the sight of the Lord, but also in the sight of men. We have sent with them our brother, whom we have often tested and found diligent in many things, but now even more diligent because of his great confidence in you. As for Titus, he is my partner and fellow worker among you; as for our brethren, they are messengers of the churches, a glory to Christ. Therefore openly before the churches, show them the proof of your love and of our reason for boasting about you" (2Co. 8:16-24).

Chapter Two

Your Obedience to Your Confession of the Gospel

"Now this I say, he who sows sparingly will also reap sparingly, and he who sows bountifully will also reap bountifully. Each one must do just as he has purposed in his heart, not grudgingly or under compulsion, for God loves a cheerful giver. And God is able to make all grace abound to you, so that always having all sufficiency in everything, you may have an abundance for every good deed; as it is written, 'HE SCATTERED ABROAD, HE GAVE TO THE POOR, HIS RIGHTEOUSNESS ENDURES FOREVER.' Now He who supplies seed to the sower and bread for food will supply and multiply your seed for sowing and increase the harvest of your righteousness; you will be enriched in everything for all liberality, which through us is producing thanksgiving to God. For the ministry of this service is not only fully supplying the needs of the saints, but is also overflowing through many thanksgivings to God. Because of the proof given by this ministry, they will glorify God for your obedience to your confession of the gospel of Christ and for the liberality of your contribution to them and to all, while they also, by prayer on your behalf, yearn for you because of the surpassing grace of God in you. Thanks be to God for His indescribable gift" (2Co. 9:6-15)!

In the Gospel of Christ

"For we are not bold to class or compare ourselves with some of those who commend themselves; but when they measure themselves by themselves and compare themselves with themselves, they are without understanding. But we will not boast beyond our measure, but within the measure of the sphere which God apportioned to us as a measure, to reach even as far as you. For we are not overextending ourselves, as if we did not reach to you, for we were the first to come even as far as you in the gospel of Christ; not boasting beyond our measure, that is, in other men's labors, but with the hope that as your faith grows, we will be, within our sphere, enlarged even more by you, so as to preach the gospel even to the regions beyond you, and not to boast in what has been accomplished in the sphere of another. But HE WHO BOASTS IS TO BOAST IN THE LORD. For it is not he who commends himself that is approved, but he whom the Lord commends" (2Co. 10:12-18).

You Have Not Received a Different Gospel

"I wish that you would bear with me in a little foolishness; but indeed you are bearing with me. For I am jealous for you with a godly jealousy; for I betrothed you to one husband, so that to Christ I might present you as a pure virgin. But I am afraid that, as the serpent deceived Eve by his craftiness, your minds will be led astray from the simplicity and purity of devotion to Christ. For if one comes and preaches another Jesus whom we have not preached, or you receive a different spirit which you have not received, or a different gospel which you have not accepted, you bear this beautifully. For I consider myself not in the least inferior to the most eminent apostles. But even if I am unskilled in speech, yet I am not so in knowledge; in fact, in every way we have made this evident to you in all things" (2Co. 11:1-6).

You Might Be Exalted, Because I Preached the Gospel

"Or did I commit a sin in humbling myself so that you might be exalted, because I preached the gospel of God to you without charge? I robbed other churches by taking wages from them to serve you; and when I was present with you and was in need, I was not a burden to anyone; for when the brethren came from Macedonia they fully supplied my need, and in everything I kept myself from being a burden to you, and will continue to do so. As the truth of Christ is in me, this boasting of mine will not be stopped in the regions of Achaia. Why? Because I do not love you? God knows I do'" (2Co. 11:7-11)!

IN THE BOOK OF GALATIANS

You Are Deserting Him for a Different Gospel

"I am amazed that you are so quickly deserting Him who called you by the grace of Christ, for a different gospel; which is really not another; only there are some who are disturbing you and want to distort the gospel of Christ. But even if we, or an angel from heaven, should preach to you a gospel contrary to what we have preached to you, he is to be accursed! As we have said before, so I say again now, if any man is preaching to you a gospel

contrary to what you received, he is to be accursed"
(Gal. 1:6-9)!

The Gospel Is Not According to Man

"For I would have you know, brethren, that
the gospel which was preached by me is not
according to man. For I neither received it from man,
nor was I taught it, but I received it through a
revelation of Jesus Christ" (Gal. 1:11-12).

I Submitted to Them the Gospel Which I Preach

"Then after an interval of fourteen years I
went up again to Jerusalem with Barnabas, taking
Titus along also. It was because of a revelation that I
went up; and I submitted to them the gospel which I
preach among the Gentiles, but I did so in private to
those who were of reputation, for fear that I might
be running, or had run, in vain. But not even Titus,
who was with me, though he was a Greek, was
compelled to be circumcised. But it was because of
the false brethren secretly brought in, who had
sneaked in to spy out our liberty which we have in
Christ Jesus, in order to bring us into bondage. But
we did not yield in subjection to them for even an
hour, so that the truth of the gospel would remain
with you. But from those who were of high
reputation (what they were makes no difference to
me; God shows no partiality) — well, those who were
of reputation contributed nothing to me. But on the
contrary, seeing that I had been entrusted with the
gospel to the uncircumcised, just as Peter had been
to the circumcised (for He who effectually worked

for Peter in his apostleship to the circumcised effectually worked for me also to the Gentiles), and recognizing the grace that had been given to me, James and Cephas and John, who were reputed to be pillars, gave to me and Barnabas the right hand of fellowship, so that we might go to the Gentiles and they to the circumcised. They only asked us to remember the poor — the very thing I also was eager to do" (Gal. 2:1-10).

They Were Not Straightforward About the Truth of the Gospel

"But when Cephas came to Antioch, I opposed him to his face, because he stood condemned. For prior to the coming of certain men from James, he used to eat with the Gentiles; but when they came, he began to withdraw and hold himself aloof, fearing the party of the circumcision. The rest of the Jews joined him in hypocrisy, with the result that even Barnabas was carried away by their hypocrisy. But when I saw that they were not straightforward about the truth of the gospel, I said to Cephas in the presence of all, 'If you, being a Jew, live like the Gentiles and not like the Jews, how is it that you compel the Gentiles to live like Jews'" (Gal. 2:11-14)?

Preached the Gospel Beforehand to Abraham

"Even so Abraham BELIEVED GOD, AND IT WAS RECKONED TO HIM AS RIGHTEOUSNESS. Therefore, be sure that it is those who are of faith who are sons of Abraham. The Scripture, foreseeing that God would justify the Gentiles by faith, preached the gospel beforehand to Abraham, saying, 'ALL THE NATIONS WILL BE BLESSED IN YOU.' So then those who are of faith are blessed with Abraham, the believer" (Gal. 3:6-9).

I Preached the Gospel to You

"I beg of you, brethren, become as I am, for I also have become as you are. You have done me no wrong; but you know that it was because of a bodily illness that I preached the gospel to you the first time; and that which was a trial to you in my bodily condition you did not despise or loathe, but you received me as an angel of God, as Christ Jesus Himself. Where then is that sense of blessing you had? For I bear you witness that, if possible, you would have plucked out your eyes and given them to me. So have I become your enemy by telling you the truth? They eagerly seek you, not commendably, but they wish to shut you out so that you will seek them. But it is good always to be eagerly sought in a commendable manner, and not only when I am present with you. My children, with whom I am again in labor until Christ is formed in you—but I could wish to be present with you now and to change my tone, for I am perplexed about you" (Gal. 4:12-20).

Chapter Two

IN THE BOOK OF EPHESIANS

The Message of Truth, the Gospel of Your Salvation

"Blessed be the God and Father of our Lord Jesus Christ, who has blessed us with every spiritual blessing in the heavenly places in Christ, just as He chose us in Him before the foundation of the world, that we would be holy and blameless before Him. In love He predestined us to adoption as sons through Jesus Christ to Himself, according to the kind intention of His will, to the praise of the glory of His grace, which He freely bestowed on us in the Beloved. In Him we have redemption through His blood, the forgiveness of our trespasses, according to the riches of His grace which He lavished on us. In all wisdom and insight He made known to us the mystery of His will, according to His kind intention which He purposed in Him with a view to an administration suitable to the fullness of the times, that is, the summing up of all things in Christ, things in the heavens and things on the earth. In Him also we have obtained an inheritance, having been predestined according to His purpose who works all things after the counsel of His will, to the end that we who were the first to hope in Christ would be to the praise of His glory. In Him, you also, after listening to the message of truth, the gospel of your salvation—having also believed, you were sealed in Him with the Holy Spirit of promise, who is given as a pledge of our inheritance, with a view to the redemption of God's own possession, to the praise of His glory" (Eph. 1:3-14).

Chapter Two

Partakers of the Promise in Christ Jesus through the Gospel

"For this reason I, Paul, the prisoner of Christ Jesus for the sake of you Gentiles—if indeed you have heard of the stewardship of God's grace which was given to me for you; that by revelation there was made known to me the mystery, as I wrote before in brief. By referring to this, when you read you can understand my insight into the mystery of Christ, which in other generations was not made known to the sons of men, as it has now been revealed to His holy apostles and prophets in the Spirit; to be specific, that the Gentiles are fellow heirs and fellow members of the body, and fellow partakers of the promise in Christ Jesus through the gospel, of which I was made a minister, according to the gift of God's grace which was given to me according to the working of His power. To me, the very least of all saints, this grace was given, to preach to the Gentiles the unfathomable riches of Christ, and to bring to light what is the administration of the mystery which for ages has been hidden in God who created all things; so that the manifold wisdom of God might now be made known through the church to the rulers and the authorities in the heavenly places. This was in accordance with the eternal purpose which He carried out in Christ Jesus our Lord, in whom we have boldness and confident access through faith in Him. Therefore I ask you not to lose heart at my tribulations on your behalf, for they are your glory" (Eph. 3:1-13).

Chapter Two

The Preparation of the Gospel of Peace

"Finally, be strong in the Lord and in the strength of His might. Put on the full armor of God, so that you will be able to stand firm against the schemes of the devil. For our struggle is not against flesh and blood, but against the rulers, against the powers, against the world forces of this darkness, against the spiritual forces of wickedness in the heavenly places. Therefore, take up the full armor of God, so that you will be able to resist in the evil day, and having done everything, to stand firm. Stand firm therefore, HAVING GIRDED YOUR LOINS WITH TRUTH, and HAVING PUT ON THE BREASTPLATE OF RIGHTEOUSNESS, and having shod YOUR FEET WITH THE PREPARATION OF THE GOSPEL OF PEACE; in addition to all, taking up the shield of faith with which you will be able to extinguish all the flaming arrows of the evil one. And take THE HELMET OF SALVATION, and the sword of the Spirit, which is the word of God" (Eph. 6:10-17).

To Make Known with Boldness the Mystery of the Gospel

"With all prayer and petition pray at all times in the Spirit, and with this in view, be on the alert with all perseverance and petition for all the saints, and pray on my behalf, that utterance may be given to me in the opening of my mouth, to make known with boldness the mystery of the gospel, for which I am an ambassador in chains; that in proclaiming it I may speak boldly, as I ought to speak" (Eph. 6:18-20).

Chapter Two
IN THE BOOK OF PHILIPPIANS

In the Defense and Confirmation of the Gospel

"I thank my God in all my remembrance of you, always offering prayer with joy in my every prayer for you all, in view of your participation in the gospel from the first day until now. For I am confident of this very thing, that He who began a good work in you will perfect it until the day of Christ Jesus. For it is only right for me to feel this way about you all, because I have you in my heart, since both in my imprisonment and in the defense and confirmation of the gospel, you all are partakers of grace with me. For God is my witness, how I long for you all with the affection of Christ Jesus. And this I pray, that your love may abound still more and more in real knowledge and all discernment, so that you may approve the things that are excellent, in order to be sincere and blameless until the day of Christ; having been filled with the fruit of righteousness which comes through Jesus Christ, to the glory and praise of God" (Php. 1:3-11).

For the Greater Progress of the Gospel

"Now I want you to know, brethren, that my circumstances have turned out for the greater progress of the gospel, so that my imprisonment in the cause of Christ has become well known throughout the whole praetorian guard and to everyone else, and that most of the brethren, trusting in the Lord because of my imprisonment, have far more courage to speak the word of God without fear. Some, to be sure, are preaching Christ even from envy and strife, but some also from good will; the latter do it out of love, knowing that I am appointed for the defense of the gospel; the former proclaim Christ out of selfish ambition rather than from pure motives, thinking to cause me distress in my imprisonment. What then? Only that in every way, whether in pretense or in truth, Christ is proclaimed; and in this I rejoice. Yes, and I will rejoice, for I know that this will turn out for my deliverance through your prayers and the provision of the Spirit of Jesus Christ, according to my earnest expectation and hope, that I will not be put to shame in anything, but that with all boldness, Christ will even now, as always, be exalted in my body, whether by life or by death. For to me, to live is Christ and to die is gain. But if I am to live on in the flesh, this will mean fruitful labor for me; and I do not know which to choose. But I am hard-pressed from both directions, having the desire to depart and be with Christ, for that is very much better; yet to remain on in the flesh is more necessary for your sake. Convinced of this, I know that I will remain and continue with you all for your progress and joy in the faith, so that your proud confidence in me may abound in Christ Jesus through my coming to you again" (Php. 1:12-26).

Striving Together for the Faith of the Gospel

"Only conduct yourselves in a manner worthy of the gospel of Christ, so that whether I come and see you or remain absent, I will hear of you that you are standing firm in one spirit, with one mind striving together for the faith of the gospel; in no way alarmed by your opponents — which is a sign of destruction for them, but of salvation for you, and that too, from God. For to you it has been granted for Christ's sake, not only to believe in Him, but also to suffer for His sake, experiencing the same conflict which you saw in me, and now hear to be in me" (Php. 1:27-30).

In the Furtherance of the Gospel

"But I hope in the Lord Jesus to send Timothy to you shortly, so that I also may be encouraged when I learn of your condition. For I have no one else of kindred spirit who will genuinely be concerned for your welfare. For they all seek after their own interests, not those of Christ Jesus. But you know of his proven worth, that he served with me in the furtherance of the gospel like a child serving his father. Therefore I hope to send him immediately, as soon as I see how things go with me; and I trust in the Lord that I myself also will be coming shortly. But I thought it necessary to send to you Epaphroditus, my brother and fellow worker and fellow soldier, who is also your messenger and minister to my need; because he was longing for you all and was distressed because you had heard that he was sick. For indeed he was sick to the point of death, but God had mercy on him, and not on him only but also on me, so that I would not have sorrow upon sorrow. Therefore I have sent him all the more eagerly so that when you see him again you may rejoice and I may be less concerned about you. Receive him then in the Lord with all joy, and hold

Chapter Two

men like him in high regard; because he came close to death for the work of Christ, risking his life to complete what was deficient in your service to me" (Php. 2:19-30).

Shared My Struggle in the Cause of the Gospel

"I urge Euodia and I urge Syntyche to live in harmony in the Lord. Indeed, true companion, I ask you also to help these women who have shared my struggle in the cause of the gospel, together with Clement also and the rest of my fellow workers, whose names are in the book of life" (Php. 4:2-3).

At the First Preaching of the Gospel

"You yourselves also know, Philippians, that at the first preaching of the gospel, after I left Macedonia, no church shared with me in the matter of giving and receiving but you alone; for even in Thessalonica you sent a gift more than once for my needs. Not that I seek the gift itself, but I seek for the profit which increases to your account. But I have received everything in full and have an abundance; I am amply supplied, having received from Epaphroditus what you have sent, a fragrant aroma, an acceptable sacrifice, well-pleasing to God. And my God will supply all your needs according to His riches in glory in Christ Jesus. Now to our God and Father be the glory forever and ever. Amen" (Php. 4:15-20).

Chapter Two
IN THE BOOK OF COLOSSIANS

In the Word of Truth, the Gospel

"We give thanks to God, the Father of our Lord Jesus Christ, praying always for you, since we heard of your faith in Christ Jesus and the love which you have for all the saints; because of the hope laid up for you in heaven, of which you previously heard in the word of truth, the gospel which has come to you, just as in all the world also it is constantly bearing fruit and increasing, even as it has been doing in you also since the day you heard of it and understood the grace of God in truth; just as you learned it from Epaphras, our beloved fellow bond-servant, who is a faithful servant of Christ on our behalf, and he also informed us of your love in the Spirit" (Col. 1:3-8).

Not Moved Away from the Hope of the Gospel

"And although you were formerly alienated and hostile in mind, engaged in evil deeds, yet He has now reconciled you in His fleshly body through death, in order to present you before Him holy and blameless and beyond reproach—if indeed you continue in the faith firmly established and steadfast, and not moved away from the hope of the gospel that you have heard, which was proclaimed in all creation under heaven, and of which I, Paul, was made a minister" (Col. 1:21-23).

Chapter Two

IN THE BOOK OF 1 THESSALONIANS

Our Gospel Came to You in Power

"We give thanks to God always for all of you, making mention of you in our prayers; constantly bearing in mind your work of faith and labor of love and steadfastness of hope in our Lord Jesus Christ in the presence of our God and Father, knowing, brethren beloved by God, His choice of you; for our gospel did not come to you in word only, but also in power and in the Holy Spirit and with full conviction; just as you know what kind of men we proved to be among you for your sake. You also became imitators of us and of the Lord, having received the word in much tribulation with the joy of the Holy Spirit, so that you became an example to all the believers in Macedonia and in Achaia. For the word of the Lord has sounded forth from you, not only in Macedonia and Achaia, but also in every place your faith toward God has gone forth, so that we have no need to say anything. For they themselves report about us what kind of a reception we had with you, and how you turned to God from idols to serve a living and true God, and to wait for His Son from heaven, whom He raised from the dead, that is Jesus, who rescues us from the wrath to come" (1Th. 1:2-10).

The Gospel of God Amid Much Opposition

"For you yourselves know, brethren, that our coming to you was not in vain, but after we had already suffered and been mistreated in Philippi, as you know, we had the boldness in our God to speak to you the gospel of God amid much opposition. For our exhortation does not come from error or impurity or by way of deceit; but just as we have been approved by God to be entrusted with the gospel, so we speak, not as pleasing men, but God who examines our hearts. For we never came with flattering speech, as you know, nor with a pretext for greed—God is witness—nor did we seek glory from men, either from you or from others, even though as apostles of Christ we might have asserted our authority. But we proved to be gentle among you, as a nursing mother tenderly cares for her own children. Having so fond an affection for you, we were well-pleased to impart to you not only the gospel of God but also our own lives, because you had become very dear to us" (1Th. 2:1-8).

We Proclaimed to You the Gospel of God

"For you recall, brethren, our labor and hardship, how working night and day so as not to be a burden to any of you, we proclaimed to you the gospel of God. You are witnesses, and so is God, how devoutly and uprightly and blamelessly we behaved toward you believers; just as you know how we were exhorting and encouraging and imploring each one of you as a father would his own children, so that you would walk in a manner worthy of the God who calls you into His own kingdom and glory" (1Th. 2:9-12).

Chapter Two

Timothy a Fellow Worker in the Gospel of Christ

"Therefore when we could endure it no longer, we thought it best to be left behind at Athens alone, and we sent Timothy, our brother and God's fellow worker in the gospel of Christ, to strengthen and encourage you as to your faith, so that no one would be disturbed by these afflictions; for you yourselves know that we have been destined for this. For indeed when we were with you, we kept telling you in advance that we were going to suffer affliction; and so it came to pass, as you know. For this reason, when I could endure it no longer, I also sent to find out about your faith, for fear that the tempter might have tempted you, and our labor would be in vain" (1Th. 3:1-5).

IN THE BOOK OF 2 THESSALONIANS

Those Who Do Not Obey the Gospel of Our Lord

"We ought always to give thanks to God for you, brethren, as is only fitting, because your faith is greatly enlarged, and the love of each one of you toward one another grows ever greater; therefore, we ourselves speak proudly of you among the churches of God for your perseverance and faith in the midst of all your persecutions and afflictions which you endure. This is a plain indication of God's righteous judgment so that you will be considered worthy of the kingdom of God, for which indeed you are suffering. For after all it is only just for God to repay with affliction those who afflict you, and to give relief to you who are afflicted and to us as well when the Lord Jesus will be revealed from heaven with His mighty angels in flaming fire, dealing out retribution to those who do not know God and to those who do not obey the gospel of our Lord Jesus. These will pay the penalty of eternal destruction, away from the presence of the Lord and from the glory of His power, when He comes to be glorified in His saints on that day, and to be marveled at among all who have believed — for our testimony to you was believed. To this end also we pray for you always, that our God will count you worthy of your calling, and fulfill every desire for goodness and the work of faith with power, so that the name of our Lord Jesus will be glorified in you, and you in Him, according to the grace of our God and the Lord Jesus Christ" (2Th. 1:3-12).

He Called You Through Our Gospel

"But we should always give thanks to God for you, brethren beloved by the Lord, because God has chosen you from the beginning for salvation through sanctification by the Spirit and faith in the truth. It was for this He called you through our gospel, that you may gain the glory of our Lord Jesus Christ. So then, brethren, stand firm and hold to the traditions which you were taught, whether by word of mouth or by letter from us" (2Th. 2:13-15).

Chapter Two

IN THE BOOK OF 1 TIMOTHY

The Glorious Gospel of the Blessed God

"But we know that the Law is good, if one uses it lawfully, realizing the fact that law is not made for a righteous person, but for those who are lawless and rebellious, for the ungodly and sinners, for the unholy and profane, for those who kill their fathers or mothers, for murderers and immoral men and homosexuals and kidnappers and liars and perjurers, and whatever else is contrary to sound teaching, according to the glorious gospel of the blessed God, with which I have been entrusted" (1Ti. 1:8-11).

IN THE BOOK OF 2 TIMOTHY

Join with Me in Suffering for the Gospel

"Therefore do not be ashamed of the testimony of our Lord or of me His prisoner, but join with me in suffering for the gospel according to the power of God, who has saved us and called us with a holy calling, not according to our works, but according to His own purpose and grace which was granted us in Christ Jesus from all eternity, but now has been revealed by the appearing of our Savior Christ Jesus, who abolished death and brought life and immortality to light through the gospel, for which I was appointed a preacher and an apostle and a teacher. For this reason I also suffer these things, but I am not ashamed; for I know whom I have believed and I am convinced that He is able to guard what I have entrusted to Him until that day. Retain the standard of sound words which you have heard from me, in the faith and love which are in Christ Jesus. Guard, through the Holy Spirit who dwells in us, the treasure which has been entrusted to you" (2Ti. 1:8-14).

Jesus Christ, Risen from the Dead, According to My Gospel

"Remember Jesus Christ, risen from the dead, descendant of David, according to my gospel, for which I suffer hardship even to imprisonment as a criminal; but the word of God is not imprisoned. For this reason I endure all things for the sake of those who are chosen, so that they also may obtain the salvation which is in Christ Jesus and with it eternal glory. It is a trustworthy statement: For if we died with Him, we will also live with Him; If we endure, we will also reign with Him; If we deny Him, He also will deny us; If we are faithless, He remains faithful, for He cannot deny Himself" (2Ti. 2:8-13).

IN THE BOOK OF PHILEMON

In My Imprisonment for the Gospel

"Therefore, though I have enough confidence in Christ to order you to do what is proper, yet for love's sake I rather appeal to you—since I am such a person as Paul, the aged, and now also a prisoner of Christ Jesus—I appeal to you for my child Onesimus, whom I have begotten in my imprisonment, who formerly was useless to you, but now is useful both to you and to me. I have sent him back to you in person, that is, sending my very heart, whom I wished to keep with me, so that on your behalf he might minister to me in my imprisonment for the gospel; but without your consent I did not want to do anything, so that your goodness would not be, in effect, by compulsion but of your own free will. For perhaps he was for this reason separated from you for a while, that you would have him back forever, no longer as a slave, but more than a slave, a beloved brother, especially to me, but how much more to you, both in the flesh and in the Lord" (Phm. 1:8-16).

IN THE BOOK OF 1 PETER

Who Preached the Gospel to You by the Holy Spirit

"As to this salvation, the prophets who prophesied of the grace that would come to you made careful searches and inquiries, seeking to know what person or time the Spirit of Christ within them was indicating as He predicted the sufferings of Christ and the glories to follow. It was revealed to them that they were not serving themselves, but you, in these things which now have been announced to you through those who preached the gospel to you by the Holy Spirit sent from heaven— things into which angels long to look" (1Pe. 1:10-12).

Chapter Two
The Gospel Has for This Purpose

"Therefore, since Christ has suffered in the flesh, arm yourselves also with the same purpose, because he who has suffered in the flesh has ceased from sin, so as to live the rest of the time in the flesh no longer for the lusts of men, but for the will of God. For the time already past is sufficient for you to have carried out the desire of the Gentiles, having pursued a course of sensuality, lusts, drunkenness, carousing, drinking parties and abominable idolatries. In all this, they are surprised that you do not run with them into the same excesses of dissipation, and they malign you; but they will give account to Him who is ready to judge the living and the dead. For the gospel has for this purpose been preached even to those who are dead, that though they are judged in the flesh as men, they may live in the spirit according to the will of God" (1Pe. 4:1-6).

Those Who Do Not Obey the Gospel of God

"Beloved, do not be surprised at the fiery ordeal among you, which comes upon you for your testing, as though some strange thing were happening to you; but to the degree that you share the sufferings of Christ, keep on rejoicing, so that also at the revelation of His glory you may rejoice with exultation. If you are reviled for the name of Christ, you are blessed, because the Spirit of glory and of God rests on you. Make sure that none of you suffers as a murderer, or thief, or evildoer, or a troublesome meddler; but if anyone suffers as a Christian, he is not to be ashamed, but is to glorify

God in this name. For it is time for judgment to begin with the household of God; and if it begins with us first, what will be the outcome for those who do not obey the gospel of God? AND IF IT IS WITH DIFFICULTY THAT THE RIGHTEOUS IS SAVED, WHAT WILL BECOME OF THE GODLESS MAN AND THE SINNER? Therefore, those also who suffer according to the will of God shall entrust their souls to a faithful Creator in doing what is right" (1Pe. 4:12-19).

IN THE BOOK OF REVELATION

Having an Eternal Gospel to Preach

"And I saw another angel flying in midheaven, having an eternal gospel to preach to those who live on the earth, and to every nation and tribe and tongue and people; and he said with a loud voice, 'Fear God, and give Him glory, because the hour of His judgment has come; worship Him who made the heaven and the earth and sea and springs of waters'" (Rev. 14:6-7).

DAILY FAITH CONFESSIONS

(These are not direct quotations from the Bible but are paraphrased confessions based on scripture.)
SAY THEM OUT LOUD.

I am God's child (Jn. 1:12). I am royalty (1 Pet. 2:9). I am hidden with Christ in God (Col. 3:3). I am united with the Lord (1 Cor. 6:17). I am a friend of Christ (Jn. 15:15). I am raised up with Him, and seated with Him in heavenly places in Christ Jesus (Eph. 2:6). I was bought with a price (1 Cor. 6:19-20). I am blessed when I come in, and blessed shall I be when I go out (Deut. 28:6). I am a personal witness of Christ (Acts 1:8). I am a saint who prays in the Holy Spirit to keep myself in the love of God (Jude 1:20-21). I draw near with confidence to the throne of grace (Heb. 4:16). I have been adopted by the Father (Eph. 1:5). I am the salt and light of the earth (Mt. 5:13). I am the head and not the tail, and I am above, and not underneath (Deut. 28:13). I have authority to trample serpents and scorpions and over all the power of the enemy (Lk. 10:19). I am a member of the body of Christ (1 Cor. 12:27). God blessed me to be fruitful, and multiply, and replenish the earth, and subdue it: and have dominion (Gen. 1:28). I cannot be separated from God's love (Ro. 8:39). The good work God has begun in me will be perfected (Phil. 1:5). I can do all things through Christ who strengthens me (Phil. 4:13). No weapon that is formed against me will prosper (Is. 54:17). So then faith cometh by hearing, and hearing by the word of God (Ro. 10:17 KJV). Faith is my currency to operate in the kingdom of God (Ro. 14:23). I am God's workmanship created in Christ Jesus for good works, which God prepared beforehand (Eph. 2:10). I have been appointed to bear fruit, and that my fruit would remain (Jn. 15:16). I am being wise when I am winning souls for King Jesus (Pr. 11:30). My body is the temple of the Holy Spirit (1 Cor. 6:19). I have access to God through the Holy Spirit (Eph. 2:18). I have been justified (Ro. 5:1). Therefore there is now no condemnation for those who are in Christ Jesus (Ro. 8:1). Greater is He who is in me than he who is in the world (1 Jn. 4:4). I will do greater works than Jesus because He went to the Father (Jn. 14:12). As God was with Moses, He will be with me; God will not fail me or forsake me (Jos. 1:5). I see myself the way God see me. God sees me as a king (Gen, 17:6, Rev. 1:6) God sees me as royalty (1 Pet. 2:9). God sees me as the righteousness of God in Christ, bold as a lion (Ro. 3:22, Pr. 28:1). God sees me without spot or wrinkle because of the blood of Jesus (1 Pet. 1:19). I am having faith for big things because God owns everything and I'm His son (Ps. 24:1). No man will be able to stand before me all the days of my life (Jos. 1:5). My Father is glorified by this that I bear much fruit, and proves I'm a disciple (see Jn. 15:8). I think big and confess big things because God is big (Ps. 24:1). I will respect God for the big God that He is and my mouth will create whatever I want (Lk. 6:45). I no longer think of millions, my renewed mind thinks of billions because the wealth of the wicked is laid up for the righteous (Pr. 13:22). The sinner's job is to gather and collect for the one who is good in God's sight (Ecc. 2:26). Redemption is not complete without prosperity. Jesus hung on the cross so I can have the whole package, not just salvation (2 Cor. 8:9). I don't have to qualify, Jesus has qualified me. Jesus reversed the curse. The devil is a liar, and Jesus is the Messiah. Jesus is made unto to me wisdom, righteousness, sanctification, and redemption (1 Cor. 1:30). I submit to God, I resist the devil and he flees from me (Jas. 4:7). For God has not given me the spirit of fear; but of power, and of love, and of a sound mind (2 Tim. 1:7). The Holy Spirit will teach me all things (Jn. 14:26). The Holy Spirit will guide me into all truth (Jn.16:13). The Holy Spirit abides in me, and I don't need anyone to teach me, but the anointing teaches me all things (1 Jn. 2:27). I quench fiery darts from the wicked one with the shield of faith (Eph. 6:16). I stand firm against the schemes of the devil (Eph. 6:11). I already have the victory and Satan cannot back me up. I hold my position of consistent victory after victory (2 Cor. 2:14). I walk in love and live by faith (Gal. 5:6). I have been redeemed from the curse of the law, poverty, sickness, and spiritual death (Gal. 3:13; Deut. 28). I will bear so much fruit. I'm God's workmanship created beforehand for good works (Eph. 2:10). God's favor is on my life (Ps. 3:8). God blesses me and His favor surrounds me as with a shield (Ps. 5:12). The kingdom of God is within me (Lk. 17:21). I have a production plant inside of me that bears fruit to change the world (Gen. 1:28). God gives me power to get wealth to establish His covenant on earth (Deut. 8:18). I am blessed to be a blessing (Gen. 12:2). I have Satan on the run. I will make a mockery of him (Jas. 4:7). I'm spending forever with King Jesus (2 Cor. 5:8)!

PRAYER FOR SALVATION

Say the following prayer out loud.

Heavenly Father, I am a sinner and I need a Savior. I confess Jesus Christ as the Lord of my life. I repent of all my sins. Father, I truly believe you raised Jesus from the dead. Father, give me spiritual hunger to spend time in Your Word day and night so my mind is renewed. I understand that by meditating and submitting to Your Word daily I will be transformed into the image of Jesus, day-by-day. Thank you, Father, for Your goodness, mercy, and grace. I pray in Jesus' name. Amen.

PRAYER FOR BAPTISM OF THE HOLY SPIRIT

Father, I am your child because Jesus is my Lord. Jesus said, "How much more shall your heavenly Father give the Holy Spirit to those who ask Him." I ask you now in the name of Jesus to fill me with the Holy Spirit. Thank you, Father, I received the baptism of the Holy Spirit by faith. I yield my vocal organs and expect to speak in tongues as the Holy Spirit gives me utterance in Jesus name. Father, I plan to pray in the Holy Spirit building myself up on my most holy faith, and keep myself in the love of God, as mentioned in Jude 20 and 21. In Jesus name I decree it. Amen.

ABOUT THE AUTHOR

Eugene Carvalho is the founder of Receiving by Faith. He is an administrator and Christian author of seventy books. God uses him in the offices of pastor, evangelist and prophet. He holds a bachelor's degree in biblical studies and a double minor in pastoral ministry and world missions. He also holds a master's degree in practical theology. Eugene prayed for a translator and God sent his wife Mercedes who has a six-year degree in Spanish from a university in Tampico, Mexico. They have participated in evangelism in the streets of Mexico for many years. They have also traveled to churches all over the United States and Mexico winning souls and preaching faith. Their current ministry website is: www.receivingbyfaith.org.

BOOKS BY EUGENE IN ENGLISH

To purchase other books by Eugene Carvalho visit receivingbyfaith.org or amazon.com.

Books in English

Receiving by Faith
Faith for Every Day: 365 Daily Devotions
Faith Cometh by Hearing, and Hearing by the Word of God
Faith, Hope, and Love
Walk in Love and Live by Faith
Topical Christian Handbook and Scripture Guide
The Gospel Is the Power of God unto Salvation
Seed Time and Harvest Time
Your New Identity in Christ
The Cross and the Blood
The Holy Spirit
The Attributes of God
The Favor of God
The Glory of God
The Grace of God
The Power of God
The Promises of God
The Throne of God
The New Testament Church
Vengeance and Recompense
God's Angel's
Prayer and Fasting
God's Mighty Prophets
A Survey of Jesus Through the Epistles

The Names of Jesus
The Psalms of David
The Righteous Will Flourish like The Palm Tree
Old Testament Miracles
New Testament Miracles
Mountain Moving Confessions
Visions and Dreams
Blessed Beyond Measure
Christ Heals: What the Bible Has to Say
My Peace I Give to You
Balancing Grace and Truth
Praise and Worship Changes Everything
Understanding the Importance of Authority
If You Are Willing and Obedient
Have Life More Abundantly
Sing Unto the Lord a New Song
The Power of the Tongue
The Supernatural: What the Bible Has to Say
The Truth Will Make You Free
Joy in the Holy Ghost
Praise Is Powerful: What the Bible Has to Say
Stewardship Regarding Our Finances
Love, Joy, and Peace Are Fruit of the Holy Ghost
Oh, Give Thanks to the Lord for He Is Good
The Kingdom of Heaven is at Hand
Acquiring Wisdom Is Vital
Grace and Mercy: What the Bible Has to Say
God Is Faithful: What the Bible Has to Say
God Is Love: What the Bible Has to Say
The God of Hope: What the Bible Has to Say
Pearls of Wisdom and Gems of Knowledge
Regarding Christianity

Victory is Mine, Joy is Mine, Peace Is Mine: I Told
Satan to Get Thee Behind
The Master's Gems
For the Kingdom of God Is Righteousness, Peace
and Joy in the Holy Ghost
Encountering Proverbs, Ecclesiastes, and Song of
Solomon Through a Topical Survey
Prayer Is Powerful: What the Bible Has to Say
My People Are Destroyed By Lack of Knowledge
Striving Toward Perfection
God Deserves Pure Worship
The Lord Requires Integrity: The Major Element of
Leadership
A Topical Look at the Book of Deuteronomy
A Topical Look at the Book of Psalms
A Topical Look at the Book of Proverbs
A Topical Look at the Book of Isaiah
A Topical Look at the Book of John
A Topical Look at the Book of Hebrews
A Topical Look at the Book of Revelation

BOOKS BY EUGENE IN SPANISH

Las Promesas de Dios
Los Salmos de David
Lo Sobrenatural: Lo que la Bíblia Tiene que Decir
Una Mirada Topica Del Libro De Los Salmos
Dios es Amor: Lo que la Biblia Tiene que Decir
La Adquisición de la Sabiduría es Vital: Lo que la
Biblia Tiene que Decir

NOTES

NOTES

<u>NOTES</u>